WITHDRAWN 11* 1/15
5-18
✗ NP

Cornerstones of Freedom

The Industrial Revolution

MARY COLLINS

CHILDREN'S PRESS®
A Division of Grolier Publishing
New York • London • Hong Kong • Sydney
Danbury, Connecticut

Visit Children's Press on the Internet at:
http://publishing.grolier.com

Library of Congress Cataloging-in-Publication Data

Collins, Mary, 1961–
    The Industrial Revolution / Mary Collins.
       p. cm.— (Cornerstones of freedom)
    Includes index.
    Summary: A history of the Industrial Revolution focusing primarily on the United
States during the nineteenth century and on the change from an agrarian society to
one based on machines and factories.
    ISBN: 0-516-21596-5 (lib. bdg.)   0-516-27036-2 (pbk.)
    1. Industrial revolution—United States Juvenile literature. 2. Industries—United
States—History Juvenile literature. 3. Inventions—United States—History Juvenile
literature. 4. Technological innovations—Economic aspects—United States—
History Juvenile literature. 5. United States—Economic conditions—To 1865
Juvenile literature. 6. United States—Social conditions—To 1865 Juvenile
literature.
    [1. Industrial revolution—United States. 2. Industries—United States—History.
3. Inventions—United States—History. 4. Technological innovations. 5. United
States—Economic conditions—To 1865. 6. United States—Social conditions—
To 1865.] I. Title.   II. Series.
HC105.C68   2000
330.973`05—dc21
                                                              99-14954
                                                                 CIP
                                                                 AC

"Revolution" means dramatic change. When the American colonists wanted to be free from British rule, they fought the American Revolution (1776–83). But there has been another kind of revolution in the world in the last two hundred years, which has influenced the way people live as much as or more than the war. Historians call it the Industrial Revolution.

It's impossible to name the precise day when this revolution began in the United States, because it's really the result of a series of changes that ended farming as the most common way of life. At the close of the American Revolution in 1783, most of the new nation's three million citizens lived on farms along the east coast. They grew their own grain, raised their own animals, such as pigs and chickens, for meat, and made their own clothes and shoes. For parents who had many children but not enough farmland, the West offered plenty of extra room for those brave enough to set out for Indian territory. The biggest American city, Philadelphia, Pennsylvania, had just forty thousand residents.

During the late 1700s, when the United States was a young nation, farming was the most common way of life for Americans.

Farm life could be grueling. The simplest of objects, such as a shirt, involved a tremendous amount of time and labor to make. First, families had to get wool either by shearing their own sheep or by buying it from someone else. Then, they had to clean and comb the wool, and spin it into thread on a spindle. Finally, the thread had to be woven into cloth on a hand loom. The final product, an itchy shirt that was often unbearably hot in the summer, was hard to wash because wool is heavy and oily. With all this hard work, it's no surprise that most people didn't own many clothes in the 1700s. The items they did own rarely were washed.

A woman spins thread on a spinning wheel. The thread she makes will likely be used to produce clothing.

Food preparation was just as difficult. Even a loaf of bread involved planting, growing, and harvesting grain, then grinding it into flour. The women in the household made dough, which they baked in a fireplace they had to keep stoked with wood—that someone else had to cut. Families often worked twelve hours a day

4

just to provide the most basic necessities. Everyone was expected to do chores, even children as young as five, who might be asked to carry water to thirsty farmworkers or to blow air on the fire using the bellows.

By 1783, people in Great Britain had already begun to make changes to escape the harsh life of a farmer.

It was common for children to help with household chores, such as cooking or cleaning.

Unlike the Americans, the British did not have an enormous amount of unsettled land. The country's population was growing but there was little new land to cultivate. Either fields had to be farmed more efficiently or people had to find another way to provide for themselves. With this problem in mind, the British began to work on ways to take advantage of their country's good roads, large number of available workers, and wealth. As a result, the Industrial Revolution took root in Great Britain first.

One of the first chores moved off the farm and into a factorylike setting was spinning and weaving. When John Kay invented a flying shuttle in 1733, it meant a thread could be passed back and forth across a loom at a much greater speed than if a person had to thread the shuttle by hand. James Hargreaves further improved the cloth-making process with his spinning jenny, which made it possible for one worker to spin eight threads at a time instead of just one. Armed with these new inventions, textile mills opened in towns across Great Britain. Now instead of working the fields

The spinning jenny, developed in the 1760s, was an improvement over the spinning wheel and flying shuttle because it could produce many threads at a time, instead of just one.

or milking the cows, young men and women could work in one of the mills for a daily wage. Then, they used the money they earned to buy, instead of make, the things they needed.

Because of the new machines, more cloth could be produced by fewer people in less time. Cotton thread was easier to use than wool. Cotton clothes were less expensive and easier to wash, which made it possible for poor people to own more clothes. These basic changes led to better hygiene, which means people were cleaner and healthier.

The interior of a cotton factory in Great Britain in the 1830s

At first a lot of the machines in the mills didn't work well, but nearly every year someone developed an improvement. By 1769, James Watt had invented the coal-powered steam engine. People had toyed with the idea of using steam as a source of power for hundreds of years, but Watt's engine was unique because it was relatively small, could be used anywhere, and could be joined to a loom or spinning jenny. Now steam power, not human muscle, could power the factory. And, unlike humans, steam never gets tired.

The closest thing that Great Britain had to mechanized power before 1769 was the waterwheel. Many mills were built along streams and rivers so that power from the flow of water could be used to push a big wheel that would then put machinery or mill stones (for grinding flour) into motion. If the water slowed because of ice or drought, the mill had to close. With Watt's machine, mill owners could set up shop anywhere without concern

Coal-powered steam engines such as this one were major advancements because they could work more efficiently than people did.

for weather conditions or water supply.

It took just thirty-six years for the British to progress from mills that relied on water power and wove yarn with Kay's flying shuttles to factories that used steam power to make cloth. That may seem like a long time, but considering that people had been living the same farm-based lifestyle for thousands of years, a few decades is a short period of time.

Waterwheels were an excellent source for powering machinery, but they could be unreliable if there wasn't enough available water to turn them.

For the people who lived in Great Britain, changes happened in stages. For many years, local women spun their own thread, brought it to the local "factory" for weaving, then brought the finished cloth home to make clothes. But by the time the daughters of these women became adults, the factory did all the steps. Instead of bringing finished yarn in for weaving, they probably just worked at the mill themselves and performed one small step in the factory process. The Industrial Revolution is unique

The work force in this late-1700s British clothing factory is made up of women and children.

among other periods when key changes took place because of the speed and number of changes that dramatically altered people's lives.

In order for this to happen, a specific set of advances had to occur. The British had to have access to plenty of coal to burn in the steam-powered engines. In the years before the opening of the textile mills, the British had improved their ability to mine and transport coal. These advances were followed by Watt's invention, which meant a factory could be built almost anywhere and fueled all year round. Improvements in the production of iron meant that machine parts could be made of material that was sturdier than wood. Even the factories, with their long corridors and grand heights (as high as four stories), couldn't be built without iron.

Great Britain tried to keep these new machines and inventions secret. The British government even passed laws that made it illegal for skilled factory workers to work in the United States. Some men, such as Samuel Slater, ignored the rules and came to the United States anyway because they thought they could make a lot of money. Slater had worked in England's textile mills. In 1790, using what he had learned in his homeland, he opened the first mechanized textile mill in the United States in Pawtucket, Rhode Island. It relied on a waterwheel for power.

Samuel Slater

Even though Americans knew about many of the dramatic changes taking place in Great Britain after the American Revolution, they weren't ready to enter into an Industrial Revolution of their own. The new country lacked a dependable transportation system, so coal from Pennsylvania couldn't always get to mills in Massachusetts. And thanks to the vast opportunities in the West, few people were willing to work ten- to twelve-hour days for just a dollar a week in a factory when they could try their luck across the Mississippi River,

In the late 1700s, thousands of Americans headed west in search of land and better opportunities.

and perhaps even get some land of their own. The combination of poor roads, few willing workers, and a lack of interest in manufacturing slowed the new country's progress in industry. In the early 1700s, Great Britain had even prohibited American colonists from producing any finished goods, such as shoes or cloth, for market. Colonists were supposed to send the raw materials, such as lumber or cotton, to Great Britain and then buy back the finished products.

This situation suited Thomas Jefferson, the third president of the United States and the author of the Declaration of Independence. He believed that the American democracy could work only if it remained a country of self-sufficient farmers who didn't need to earn wages. "The American people will be more virtuous, more free and more happy employed in agriculture than as carriers or manu-facturers," he wrote.

Thomas Jefferson

Alexander Hamilton, the United States's first Secretary of the Treasury, disagreed with Jefferson and believed that if the United States was to be truly independent of Great Britain it would have to manufacture its own goods. "Why all this opposition to our working up those materials that God and nature have given us? What countries are the most flourishing and most powerful in the world? Manufacturing countries."

Alexander Hamilton

Americans began to side with Hamilton's point of view during the War of 1812. Great Britain and France were battling over trading rights and U.S. ships kept getting caught in the middle. The British harassed the Americans by boarding and searching their ships and even seizing U.S. sailors. This resulted in the former colonies declaring war on Great Britain. During the war, the flood of British imports stopped. No more shiploads of cotton cloth, clocks, shoes, tools, and other goods came to American shores. If Americans wanted these products, they would have to manufacture them on their own. Even though the war lasted a short time, it gave American industry an excellent opportunity. By 1814, the first steam-powered textile mill opened in Waltham, Massachusetts. It was followed less than ten years later by the now-famous textile mills of Lowell, Massachusetts. The Industrial Revolution was finally in full swing in the United States.

A cotton mill in Lowell, Massachusetts, one of many signs that the Industrial Revolution had arrived in the United States

Both the United States and Great Britain experienced strong opposition to the social changes that resulted from industrialization. Perhaps the most dramatic and well-known rebels were the Luddites. The Luddites were a group of angry British artisans who believed that factory life, with its tedious repetition, low wages, long hours, and dull environment, deprived them of the chance to continue their own more creative way of work.

For centuries, skilled craftsmen had created finished products one by one and taught their skills to young boys called apprentices. Sometimes they worked at their crafts full-time, but just as often they worked at them as side jobs, with many family members taking part in the production process. They'd work in the fields, come back to a small shed and do some stitch work on a set of shoes, then head to the house for something to eat. There were no clocks or factory bosses. Most adults worked twelve-hour days, but much of that time was spent outside. They were able to do a variety of tasks, not just one specific job, the way people in factories worked. They also could work on a project from beginning to end, but a millworker had nothing to do with any other part of production and rarely saw or cared about the finished product.

For hundreds of years, the most common way of learning a trade or craft was through apprenticeship.

Once the factories began selling goods produced in large quantities for low prices, the independent weavers, shoemakers, and other artisans could not compete. To fight back, the Luddites broke into factories at night and smashed machines. During the first few raids, they met with little resistance. But news of their efforts spread throughout Great Britain. Preoccupied with a war overseas, the British government had no patience for the actions of the Luddites. The government began arresting and hanging men accused of wrecking machines. For two years, the Luddites battled on, but over time the harsh penalties they suffered and the tremendous success of the factory system defeated them.

By the end of the Luddite movement in 1814, British industry was well situated to take the next big step in the Industrial Revolution: railroads. In both the United States and Great Britain, steamboats and elaborate canal systems had greatly improved the ability of commercial goods and people to travel long distances. Robert Fulton and Robert Livingston launched the first safe, regular

The Luddites sometimes ambushed and murdered factory owners who introduced machinery into their factories.

steamboat service in the United States when
they fired up the boiler of the *Clermont* on the
Hudson River in New York in 1807. Locals
cheered when the awkward boat covered 150
miles (241 kilometers) in thirty-two hours!

But what the steamboats and canal systems
could do, the railroad could do even better.
Trains didn't need water, which meant they
could carry goods and passengers anywhere
engineers could set a rail. Until 1814, the
problem had been producing rails that could
withstand the weight of a railroad car without
becoming brittle. Due to some important
advances in the iron-making process, the British
were the first to produce the reliable rails
necessary for long train lines.

*Canal systems
enabled barges and
steamboats to
transport goods
and people.*

When George Stephenson's *Rocket* won a national contest in Great Britain for best locomotive design in 1829, he opened the door to smooth-running, steam-powered, long-distance travel. Eager to get their hands on the latest train model, a new railroad and canal company, the Camden and Amboy of New Jersey, sent Robert Stevens to Great Britain to study Stephenson's designs. Stevens was so impressed he ordered the *John Bull* from Stephenson's factory. The steam-powered passenger train was put into service along the New York–Philadelphia line in 1831. It marked the beginning of a huge boom in railroad building. The locomotive helped Americans reach across their immense landscape. It made it possible to build cities, including Chicago, Illinois, and San Francisco, California. During the next thirty years, thousands of miles of railroad tracks were laid. Private companies and state governments began improving roads.

The vast transportation network that had proved so essential to Great Britain's own Industrial Revolution was finally being laid in the United States. Raw materials could be carried to factories, and finished goods could be

When the John Bull *went into service in 1831, it was so successful that plans were made to build even more railroad lines.*

During the mid-1800s, railroad tracks were constructed throughout the country.

taken to markets quickly and cheaply. Coal and iron, two important resources, were plentiful. Throughout the country, industry began to expand at a remarkable rate. Just fifty years after winning independence from Great Britain, the United States was manufacturing enough goods to meet its own needs. By the late 1800s, it had become one of the largest industrial nations in the world.

With the coming of the railroad and factory culture, people had to worry about getting places on time. They no longer could get up with the sun, do their chores at their own pace, and then go to bed at sundown. Suddenly people needed timepieces.

The story of the clock industry in the United States illustrates the trends of the Industrial Revolution in this country. Other than a few shopkeepers, no one in the colonies had owned a clock in the early 1700s. The rhythms of nature, not machines, set the work pace.

Eli Terry

In 1802, Eli Terry, a clock maker in Plymouth, Connecticut, began making clocks with wooden wheels. Terry made three to four clocks a year for his small number of interested customers. To improve his production, he developed a water-powered tool that helped him cut the wheels for the inner workings of the clock at a much faster pace. He began producing as many as two hundred clocks a year, which he gave to a peddler to sell in the countryside.

Each year, Terry found other ways to speed production until he and his coworkers were making seventy-five clocks a day! But even at this rate, Terry and the other clock makers could not keep up with the booming demand for timepieces. By 1845, clock making moved out of the small shops like his and into the factory, where unskilled workers made and assembled clocks at a much faster rate than Terry could. Few, if any, of the factory workers knew how the entire clock mechanism worked. With the help of steam power, sharp metal tools, and metal parts, a factory could produce 100,000 clocks a year that cost less than $2 each. Soon nearly every American home contained a clock.

From 1861 to 65, the American Civil War slowed industrialization in some areas, especially the South, which was already far behind the North in its shift from a farming culture to an industry-based one. But the armies of the North

Clock factories such as this one took business away from skilled craftsmen like Eli Terry because factory workers could produce more clocks in less time than Terry could.

and the South also created a great demand for mass-produced goods, from food to clothing and guns. Many merchants who had set up factories made a fortune during the war and used their profits to launch what many historians call a Second Industrial Revolution in the United States. Andrew Carnegie was just such a businessman. He used profits he made during and after the war to create one of the most successful industries in the country: Carnegie Steel.

Andrew Carnegie

Born and raised in Scotland until the age of eleven, young Andrew Carnegie emigrated to Pittsburgh, Pennsylvania, with his parents and brother in 1844. To survive, everyone in the family had to find a way to make money, even the boys. Their father was a hand weaver, the kind of artisan the Industrial Revolution was quickly putting out of business, so he didn't have much money. Their mother found work making shoes. Carnegie himself worked in a textile mill ten hours a day changing bobbins. During the next few years, he moved from the mill to a job at the railroad. He built a reputation for hard work and intelligence and, by the age of twenty, he was superintendent of the local railroad.

Andrew Carnegie jumped from his railroad job to his life as one of the wealthiest men in the

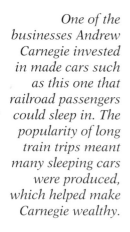

One of the businesses Andrew Carnegie invested in made cars such as this one that railroad passengers could sleep in. The popularity of long train trips meant many sleeping cars were produced, which helped make Carnegie wealthy.

United States because he invested his money in other businesses. If the companies did well, they gave him a portion of the profits, called a dividend. By age twenty-eight, Carnegie had earned so much money from dividends that he no longer had to work in an office. He didn't return to regular company work until 1872, when he launched Carnegie Steel. Now he not only had money in the company, he ran it!

Steel was much sturdier than iron and quickly became the preferred metal for the railroads. Steel rods from Carnegie's company were used in the construction of the Brooklyn Bridge and the Washington Monument. His business was soon worth millions of dollars.

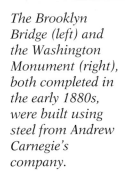

The Brooklyn Bridge (left) and the Washington Monument (right), both completed in the early 1880s, were built using steel from Andrew Carnegie's company.

This photograph of factory workers in New York City was taken during the 1890s.

But Carnegie Steel's good, inexpensive product came at a high price. The men who worked in the intensely hot, noisy factory earned low wages for their dangerous labor. If they got hurt or sick and couldn't work, they didn't get paid. In the 1870s, workers didn't have health insurance, paid vacations, or sick leave, which are common benefits for today's workers.

This profit-oriented approach to work existed in nearly every American business by the late 1800s, especially in mining, garment working, textile mills, and steel. Some workers felt powerless. Industry had revolutionized their lives. They had better clothes, running water, easier ways to travel, more food, mass-produced shoes, clocks, kitchen tools, blankets, and more. But they had less control over their daily lives. They had to be at their jobs at a specific time and work all day under the careful eye of a supervisor. They could use the money they earned to buy their bread instead of making it themselves. But they also spent less time with their families and could make fewer decisions about their daily routines.

By the 1900s, workers began fighting to revolutionize the workplace once again, but this time in their favor. They joined together in large groups, called unions, and threatened to stop work if the company owners didn't improve their working conditions and wages. Sometimes things became violent, when businessmen such as Andrew Carnegie refused to give in. Workers battled in factory yards and filed lawsuits against their employers in an effort to assert their rights. Today the results of these hard-fought battles can be seen in the five-day work week, paid sick leave, safer work environments, and better opportunities for women and minorities.

By the early 1900s, factory workers commonly went on strike to demand higher pay and better working conditions.

By 1920, the United States had officially become a country of cities and towns instead of farms. Most people had moved from the farm fields to a world that included cars, electric lights, huge cities, and an endless amount of factory-made goods. In Detroit, Michigan, Henry Ford's automobile factory was assembling one new car every ninety minutes.

It took another Scotsman with a viewpoint different from Andrew Carnegie's to point out the disadvantages of Americans' need to make and consume products. Like Carnegie, John Muir emigrated to the United States as a young boy. Instead of settling in an industrial town

Henry Ford sits in the driver's seat of one of the cars produced at his automobile factory in Detroit, Michigan.

such as Pittsburgh, however, Muir's family moved to the woods of Wisconsin, where they barely survived as farmers.

Young John Muir escaped the drudgery of his life in Wisconsin by taking a job as a mechanic for a steamboat, and later, in a broom factory. Oddly enough, the future founder of the environmental movement in the United States was good with machines and was an ideal factory worker. But one day a metal file flew into his eye, temporarially blinding him. He recovered his sight but quit his job. He vowed to spend the rest of his days exploring the wonders of the country's natural landscape and doing what he could to save it from further destruction. He saw the great forests and fields of the United States as rare treasures worth saving, not as raw materials for industry.

John Muir

The great machines that powered the Industrial Revolution used up enormous amounts of natural resources and polluted the air and water. The tremendous surge in industrial development also took its toll on people's health. Hazardous work conditions sometimes led to life-threatening injuries, and sooty air weakened lungs and made workers more susceptible to diseases, such as pneumonia or bronchitis. People who lived near the city smokestacks often suffered similar problems, even if they didn't work in the factories, because the overall air quality was so poor. Because it was costly to make any changes in the manufacturing process, companies were slow to admit that pollution was bad for the environment and people's health. The government was slow to pass pollution-control laws. Today, while the United States continues to struggle with the pollution problems that result from living in an industrialized society,

Industrial pollution takes a toll on the environment and people's health.

the government has passed stricter pollution laws. People are more aware of industrial pollution and the need to control it.

As a new century begins, the United States faces yet another revolution: the Computer Age. The dramatic changes in how information is gathered and processed have altered nearly every aspect of day-to-day life, in the same way that the mechanized mills changed every step of the cloth-making process. In some ways, computers have brought the worker full circle by making it easier to work at home once again. Anyone can operate a business out of their house, thanks to e-mail, faxes, phones, computers, and other machines that rely on modern technology. Who knows where this revolution will carry us?

An employee at work in his home office

GLOSSARY

apprentice

A spindle is part of a spinning wheel.

apprentice – someone who learns a trade or craft by working with a skilled person

artisan – someone who is skilled at working with his or her hands at a particular craft

bobbin – a spool on which yarn or thread is wound

bellows – an instrument or device whose sides are squeezed to pump air into something such as an organ or a fire

emigrate – to leave your own country in order to live permanently in another one

imports – merchandise from a foreign country

labor – physical work

manufacturing – making goods from raw materials, usually with machines

market – a place where people buy and sell goods

mill – a building or factory equipped with machinery for processing a material, such as paper, textiles, or steel

peddler – someone who travels around selling things

profit – the amount of money left after all the costs of operating a business have been subtracted from all the money earned

raw material – a substance, such as wood or leather, that is processed and made into a useful finished product

spindle – the round stick or rod on a spinning wheel that holds and winds thread

tedious – tiring and boring

union – a group of workers who try to get better wages and working conditions

wages – the money someone is paid for his or her work

TIMELINE

John Kay invents the flying shuttle **1733**

1764

James Watt invents the **1769**
modern steam engine

James
Hargreaves
invents the
spinning jenny

1776
⎫ American Revolution
1783

1790 Slater's Mill opens
in Pawtucket,
Rhode Island

Clermont begins service **1807**
on the Hudson River

1811
War of 1812 **1812** ⎫ Luddites riot in England
leads to U.S. **1814**
manufacturing First steam-powered textile mill
boom **1815** opens in Waltham, Massachusetts

George Stephenson's *Rocket* **1829**
wins contest in Great Britain **1831** The *John Bull* begins service

1845 Clock making mostly done in factories

1861
⎫ American Civil War
1865

Railroad tracks span the country **1869**

1872 Carnegie Steel opens in Pittsburgh,
Pennsylvania

1900

1920 For the first time, more Americans live in
cities rather than on farms

Workers strike to
improve working
conditions

INDEX *(Boldface page numbers indicate illustrations.)*

PHOTO CREDITS

Photographs ©: American Clock & Watch Museum: 20; Archive Photos: 6, 24, 31 top; Brown Brothers: 22; Cameramann International, Ltd.: 29; Corbis-Bettmann: 9 (Hubert Stadler), cover, 1, 11, 14, 15, 17, 28, 30 top; Holt-Atherton Department of Special Collections: 27; Liaison Agency, Inc.: 2, 8, 10, 23 left, 26 (Hulton Getty); Mary Evans Picture Library: 7, 16; Museum of the City of New York: 21 bottom (Archive Photos); North Wind Picture Archives: 5, 12, 13 top, 18, 19, 25, 31 bottom; Stock Montage, Inc.: 3, 4, 13 bottom, 21 top, 30 bottom; Visuals Unlimited: 23 right (Jeff Greenberg).

PICTURE IDENTIFICATIONS

Cover Photo: Factory workers in La Salle, Illinois, in 1889; Title Page: Factory workers at the Ford Motor Company in 1913; Page 2: An American farm in about 1775

ABOUT THE AUTHOR

Mary Collins works as an editor for National Geographic *World* Magazine and as a freelance writer for a variety of publications. She has written several titles for the Cornerstones of Freedom series, including *Mount Vernon, The Smithsonian Institution,* and *The Spanish-American War.* She lives in Alexandria, Virginia.